(Re)Creations

(Re)Creations

poems by

Phyllis H. Meshulam

© 2025 Phyllis H. Meshulam. All rights reserved.
This material may not be reproduced in any form, published,
reprinted, recorded, performed, broadcast,
rewritten, or redistributed without
the explicit permission of Phyllis H. Meshulam.
All such actions are strictly prohibited by law.

Cover design by Shay Culligan
Cover image by Jerry Meshulam
Author photo by Jerry Meshulam

ISBN: 978-1-63980-680-5

Kelsay Books
502 South 1040 East, A-119
American Fork, Utah 84003
Kelsaybooks.com

First and foremost, to my family: my husband, whose responsibilities have increased perhaps a thousandfold during my illness and our daughters who have been so supportive in whatever way they can, coming and visiting and actually helping with this manuscript!

To Terry Ehret, who really saved my tenure as poet laureate by volunteering to be co-editor for the county anthology.

Last but definitely not least, to Jodi Hottel who has taken it upon herself, in conjunction with my daughter, Audrey, to see this project come to fruition.

Acknowledgments

Thanks to the following organizations where some of these poems were previously published:

Artemis Journal: "Who Came First"
Bullets into Bells Website: "Infringed"
Crow, in the Light of Day, in the Dark of Night: "Daughters," "Scattered"
Dancing Poetry Festival: "I Promise" (3rd Place Award, 2018), "Un Niño Que Ha Llorado" (3rd Place Award, 2019), "A New Quilt for Martin Luther King Jr." (3rd Place Award, 2023)
Fruit of Life: "Templo del Sol"
Marin Poetry Center Anthology: "Between Hourglass and Sea," "Seeds," "What the Willow Saw"
Off the Page Readers' Theater Production: "Un Niño Que Ha Llorado"
Phoenix, Out of the Silence—And Then: "Chapel," "Fire Dragon," "Ghosts"
Poets of the Vineyards Newsletter: "Hanuman, Monkey God"
San Diego Poetry Annual: "Jokes"
Sebastopol Living: "Planet of the Apples," "One Boy Who Cried," "A New Quilt for Martin Luther King Jr.," "Goddess's Dream," "In Wilderness"
Sonoma County Magazine: "Away from the Reports"
Twist in Time: "Eriksython"
Veterans Writing Group Quarterly: "Wings," "Swift Water"

And thanks to Lisa Gluskin Stonestreet and members of the mostly Monday writers' group for their help editing these poems.

For additional help with editing, thanks to the Poets of the Vineyard.

Thanks to Jackie Hallerberg and Judy Cheung for organizing the above groups respectively, and, along with John Johnson and Mary Lindberg, for their wonderful friendship in the time of my illness!

Contents

I. (Re)Creations

Goddess's Dream	19
Templo del Sol	20
A Woman Fell Up to the Sky	21
Initiation	23
Hanuman, Monkey God	25
Who Came First?	26
Morning, Galápagos Islands	27
Eden?	28
Eliana's Bat Mitzvah	29
Seeds	31
Philomela	32
Erysikthon	34
Mothers, Daughters, Sisters	36
Legacy of the Drunken Sailor	38
After the Flood, God Makes a Mental Note	40
Infringed	41
Thirteen Ways of Looking at the Calendar	42

II. Firebird on a Changing Globe

Oh, Gulf	47
Firebird Suite	49
Fire Dragon	54
Ravenous Water	55
Monarchs	57
Seeing the Light	58
Wings	59
In a Galaxy We Call Home	61
Slothful	62
Between Hourglass and Sea	63

Planet of the Apples	65
Madre de Dios River	66
Earth Works	68
In Wilderness	70
Variations on a Theme of Green	71

III. Spirit of Justice

A New Quilt for Martin Luther King Jr.	75
The Story	77
Sanctuary	78
Scattered	80
Un Niño Que Ha Llorado	82
Asylum Seekers	84
Deportation 1 (out of 975 so far)	85
Among Many Days of the Dead	86
Lumps	88
Dear Editor	89
Christine (Blasey Ford)	91
Congressional Pirates?	92
A Book of Ruths	94
Jokes	96
I Promise	97
Mouse of Enlightenment	98

I. (Re)Creations

Goddess's Dream

The black new moon of my belly is set
in a crescent of shine, and from it
a boy, a girl will soon come forth,
more or less in my image, of course.

They now are fish-like; may they always recall
their slick gill-slits. Come their time to crawl
may they be tutored by beetles and moles.
Their time to run, likewise by deer and a foal.

May my daughter grow strong as my son
never shoved from her place in the sun.
For I have dreamed of weeping women
and deadly warriors, and have seen

the universe split open, crack into stars:
into Venus, teardrop, blood-drop of Mars.

Templo del Sol

Machu Picchu, dawn

Who is coming along the underside of night

who has fractured the obsidian mountains
      and gilded their brokenness
Only the Inca wrens
        and birds of dawn
Only the Urubamba River   gabbling and rumbling
do not stand mute

Who has thrown up camel-hump mountains, filigreed with green
    The valley boiling cool with salt-mists
It is you
    The carved-water mirrors stand ready
    The matchmakers of stone have assembled

                this city
          this courtyard   these terraces
          this temple   this dark trapezoidal
                                passage
      for you
A cloud flutters prostrate

It is you
      whose image we carry in our core
      You who chlorophylls the tree stars

The very rock we stand on
              once diaphanous in your embrace

Beyond the shining blade-ledge of night

it is you appearing

      there   there
                            over there

A Woman Fell Up to the Sky

in the Dolomites

A woman looked up to peaks and
thought, if they were hers to name,
she would call this one, "Helmet of the Great War,"
and those, "Crayola Box Spires."
Saw the book of the world,
histories in each striation, rulers, fools, ruler-fools,
ink-green pines, velvet-green meadows,
dandelion yellow, gentian blue,
loose-strife flowers in purple abandon.
She saw places where ice barracks and trenches once were.
Saw the museum where mannequins with identical faces
wear uniforms of gas mask enemies.
Not that this is sadder than foes with mismatched faces,
but it goes to show how men will be enemies.
Later the woman fell up to the sky,
found herself in mountains then rubbed
in night-time gray, halfway to heaven
with the faintest feeling of wings.
Wondered where the sun would appear
as her world rolled toward it.
Found a turtle cloud to be her guide
who showed her a starfish fossil on a peak.
Saw the mountains of many faces:
the sneezer, the dreamer,
the devil with long canine teeth,
a bishop in mitre and robes, owl,
leopard—all equals.
Wondered why we try to find
our likenesses in immensity.
She saw no woman's face and
felt how much she doubts herself.

Then found her mirror in the fluxing of clouds,
snake to scarf, sometimes nestling,
sometimes sneaking.
Saw the clouds glow rosewater,
then mango, then buttered milk.
She decides to fly back to ground,
feels like a bird
looking only for the right branch
to be her land.

Initiation

More than half-way through the journey of my life,
I have discovered a path and taken a task.

Hot January afternoon, unblinking sun,
and I am homesick for winter.
Homesick, too, for the shade
of my childhood's backyard tree
in whose roots and branches
I am often tangled in dreams.
Maybe I can climb—not the tree,
there is no tree here—but
the faint zigzag of wispy clouds.

I am a seeker—
wondering what to do
about this taut lens of dry air
that puts my piece of the planet
under a burning magnifying glass.
And I am compelled by tales
of the cauldron-born bard, and
of the Old One who brews rosemary and sage
into Her tonics, Her truths.

The switch-backs of clouds are steep,
granite-dusty. Of course
I fall—why am I always falling?—
grating my shins, breathing the dust,
twisting my walking sticks.
Thirsty for rain, I persist

until I stand, blistering
before the heat waves of a bronze cauldron,
askew in space.

I peer inside.
There She is!
—in a molten mirror.

Hanuman, Monkey God

Part of the Ramayana epic, as danced by the Khon Masked Dance Troupe at the Sala Chalemkrung Royal Theatre in Bangkok

Hanuman, typical trickster, can't
resist the fruits in Phra Uma's garden.
He shakes her trees, gobbles plums,
does somersaults in glee.
She is not amused.
Her curse depletes his strength.

He slinks off, humbled monkey,
tail between legs, to seek Rama's favor.
Rama does need a tricky ally right now,
seeking to regain his wife, the goodliest
goddess Sita, from the demon-god, Ravana.

What do you do with a problem
like Ravana? Many arms to point the way,
many heads to show he's smart, but
so full of himself he challenged gods,
then wifenapped Sita from Rama.
Female as pawn

Although, was it partly because Rama
had cut off Ravana's sister's nose?
Another female as pawn

I don't get it, but Hanuman sure was cute—
and all he did was eat forbidden fruit.

Who Came First?

Against all evidence, the Bible says
"Man did not come from woman but woman
came from man." Excuse me, what did you say?
Oh, wait a sec. I think I understand.

It's pregnancy envy. The authors fibbed:
God gave Adam a spinal block, performed
Cesarean section, removed a rib
and from it, another human was formed.

But lesser, fe-male, wo-man, infantile,
of course. To be seen, not heard, and servile,
obedient, useful. Eve had different
ideas, for sure. So, she took forbidden

fruit and ate. She listened to the earthiest
of creatures. Turned subservient to subversive.

Morning, Galápagos Islands

Life has dreamed up red feet,
unlikely as they are bright,
flexible, webbed, made to wrap
around a branch. Boobies
in all their stages. Snowball chick
with black snorkel mask.
Hatchling, plucked, gray, wormlike.
Tucked by mother into the comfort
of her yuca dumpling breast.

Stages of evolution, too. Blue feet,
gray feet, red. Blue beaks,
blue eyeliner. This one steps gingerly
sideways then disappears into leafy twigs
when I glance away—at black cliffs,
horizon robed in blue, gravelly sand.
Seems like the peaceable
kingdom here, with orange-frilled
frigate youth in adjacent nests.
But frigates must thieve to survive.
Among blue and gray boobies, every
second egg, by fratricide, is doomed.

Early last century, entered two Adams,
with their Eves, fleeing threats and effects of war.
Ritter and Wittmer ended up more like Cain and Abel.

I feel I've seen morning in Eden here,
so close to creation. But what do I mean by Eden?
Not paradise but a hatchery for life in all its prisms?

Eden?

Sunday lunch
in a backyard full of fallen fruit,
the air rich with nosegays
of cinnamon and cider.

He wonders aloud
if more of this bounty
could have been collected
to feed the hungry.

She rises
and brings him
an apple from the tree.
Paradise

in a piece of fruit—Gravenstein—
more gold than green,
with splashes
of true ruby.

Just a woman
and a man
sharing an apple
on a summer afternoon.

Eliana's Bat Mitzvah

> *... God tested Abraham. And He said to him ..., "Take, pray, your son ..., Isaac ..., and offer him up as a burnt offering ..."*
> —Genesis Chapter 22: 1, 2, tr. Robert Alter

She's only thirteen
but she can imagine
the betrayal the mother felt
when God demanded—
and Abraham agreed—
he sacrificed their son—
that child who took
so long to conceive—
that Sarah was sure she
never would be a mother.

A life and a parent's love crushed
for a display of obedience?

The thirteen-year-old,
ready to become a woman,
having studied her delegated
Torah portion, wrote and now shares
a letter from Sarah's point of view,
wondering if both God and
Abraham knew that the former
never would follow through.

But, Abraham, our child?
How did he feel on that pile
of kindling? Oh, God, why?

This test: a threat to
life and love, and psyche.

Maybe because Eliana lost her best
friend to brain cancer in fifth grade,
she knows—beyond her years—
how Sarah felt,
how any mother would.

Seeds

And it happened . . . that God tested Abraham.

Pine torch and tinder at hand,
I ask, ". . . where is the sheep for the offering?"
(For that matter, where is my half-brother Ishmael?)
"God will see to the sheep," Dad replied.

Dad has always preached obedience,
and tells me to lie down. I lay my body on
kindling thick with lichen. And
whatever might have happened next,
a gust of wind interrupted
and Dad said to get up. I obeyed.

I later learned that God had blessed my dad's
obedience, and promised seed multiplying like stars.

I see now I'm a seed. So is Ishmael.
God also promised Father the power to storm
his enemies' gates. I see some of my seeds
becoming enemies to some of Ishmael's.
And our children storming each other's gates.

Philomela

It writhed like a snake
on the ground, the tongue of the woman
raped by her brother-in-law.
Then maimed to keep her quiet.
Held silent in a distant palace.
She will weave a cloth from her tale,
stitch a loophole in the NDA.
Surely someone will read
these symbols that explain the pain
make the case for her right to her tongue.

>   Why do I still doubt myself?
>   Can I silence the inner critic
>   and my memories of its allies?
>   Every half-filled journal, a reproach.
>   "Don't stain the family name."
>   A cautionary tale from Dad went:
>   "She thought she was getting
>   a poem published—and she was—but
>   it was included in a section on how
>   not to write a poem."

And Philomela, how does her story end?
All the characters turned to birds.
About to take revenge on the sisters' revenge,
her assailant turns into a hoopoe.
Black-and-white striped nethers, fiery headdress,
sword becomes a long thin beak.

Forever chanting *hoop hoop*.
The girl whose song he stopped, meanwhile,
is a nightingale—rufous, round, petite.
Her throbbing throat trills pearls of song
on throughout the night.

Erysikthon

1.

A many-turreted tree, sacred to holy Ceres,
twig-fingers webbed with new green,
draped in prayer flags.
But he will have none of that.
For lumber and his empire, it will be dispatched.
"Foreman, henchmen, bring it down!
Who cares for the curse of its resident nymph?
I will build the finest feast hall,
the polish, the sheen of its hardwood floors.
The glossy tables with an inner flame
captured in their woody grain.
The dazzling chandeliers."

2.

"Sir, I cannot chop it," the foreman says.
"You will, or I'll chop you," he tells him, and does.
Man and tree alike shed human blood.
The nymph calls out her curse, then calls on Ceres,
goddess of grain and plenty, who summons
the shriveled wraith, Hunger, to inhabit the king.

3.

"Hunger, hungah—mine—stirs, burns.
Platterful of quail, their toothpick bones slide down.
And the cavern opens again.
Platterful of roast goat—consumed!
Sell the platter, after licking off its grease.
Sell the feast hall for a few more feasts.
And when the oxen are gone, dismembered
limb by limb, their blood all drunk for wine,
the last goblet filled, drained, sold
for the price of one last pour,
sell the daughter as a slave. Her anklets
fetch an extra price.
And when all that is gone,
what of this fine-furry arm?
I cry in pain when I bite it, but it must
be shoveled into the roaring furnace
of my gut. What of this muscled leg?"

Mothers, Daughters, Sisters

The mother is no parent of that which is called her child
but only nurse of the new-planted seed that grows.
The parent is he who mounts . . .
—Aeschylus, *Eumenides*

    1.

Sisters   sisters   sisters,
  you float your tunics,
togas, skirts, pantaloons
  across millennia.
Your powers snuffed, your deities dethroned,
  minds smothered under assumptions, traditions, many based,
like the judgment of Apollo, on propaganda
  disguised as courtroom drama
in which the judge denies even maternity,
      demotes you to nurse of the child that you have borne.

    2.

Here's the deal: Agamemnon assembled an army
      brought them to the grim, gray, harsh rocks of a coast.
To the glass-blown ocean heaving and revealing, but with no wind
  to snag the sails. The men grew restless as waves, so Ag
appealed to the gods. Artemis answered. Said
  nothing would do but to sacrifice his daughter,
a pearl of a girl who must die on the pyre, so the war
  effort could move forward. Ten years.
Agamemnon survived the war but not the plot
      by his wife and her lover to avenge the girl.

But wife did not survive vengeance either, meted out by
    their son. The Furies were furious over the matricide, but
    Apollo—
him again—defanged them with his judgment.

    3.

Woman, if you (my mother, let's say) want
    to be the judge, captain,
playwright, poet, philosopher?
    What if you seek to author more than
Golden Books, cookbooks; paint more than
    the canvas of your face;
create something that will last
    longer than dinner?

If you fail, but at least bear a daughter
    want for her what
you could not achieve,
    you may be doomed to watch
her hesitant steps
    stop at what she deems her limit,
in dancers' shoes,
    as she cries out, "I am crippled
by my blues."

Legacy of the Drunken Sailor

They say Noah was a righteous man and
600 years old at the time of the flood.
What do I make of this when I know the rest?
That once the waters drew back, he planted a vineyard,
with all its green to crimson leaves, green to purple
grapes, made wine, got drunk, and passed out naked.

Still, maybe, Noah was a righteous man, but that wasn't all.
Ham saw his father and told his brothers about daddy bare.
Those two backed up to their father, and threw a woven
robe over him, never seeing his pale, unclothed body.
Noah, that righteous man, awoke from his stupor and knew
exactly whom to blame. So Noah cursed Ham or, in fact,
cursed his grandson, Canaan, Ham's son,
saying he would be a lowly slave to all the rest.

Talk about the "sins" of the father being visited on the son!
Or the sins of the grandfather visited on the grandson.
But Noah was a righteous man.

Around the early Mediterranean,
all foreign and conquered peoples were enslaved.
But Black Africans made an easy "other."

Later, blending ancient languages like grapes for wine,
the willing decided that *ham* meant "black or sooty."
Sloppy etymology, most now say.

Are we still living with this?
A "righteous" man says the election was stolen
(too many "sooty" people voted) and legislatures
leap into action, making it harder to vote,
especially for those without a car, or working
long hours.

Noah lived 950 years so—you'd think—
a righteous man would have gained some wisdom by then.
Or maybe he (like the rest of us, righteous or not)
was just slow to learn.

After the Flood, God Makes a Mental Note

*. . . and the Lord said in His heart, "I will not
again damn the soil on humankind's score."*

And maybe,
to instruct humankind,
I should set
a better example

Infringed

A morning dawns, barely, with fringes of rain along
the *well*-worn path to the daily paper.
Regulated by her body's clock, still on Eastern time,
Melissa dodges the drops, dribble and splat.
Being home from her trip
makes it *necessary* to re-enter routine,
to plan her lessons, pay her bills.
take out *the* trash. She finds
security in these habits. But the news announces another
shooting *of* innocents by a madman with
a gun. "How exactly does this make us
free?" she wonders. It leaves her
in a *state* of bewilderment.
The paper also mentions
a gun-*rights*-advocating family in Nevada, still grieving at the bedside
of their wife/mother/sister, victim
of *the* Vegas concert shooting where
58 *people* were killed, 489 wounded. Like Rosemarie who struggles
to keep food down,
keep family morale up,
and for whom anti-anxiety drugs are now an essential nutrient.
They *bear* it by crying in each other's
arms, remembering the fun-lover their matriarch was,
so that person *shall*
not perish from this earth. They come to realize that her right
to *be* intact has been
infringed by the blast effect of high-speed bullets and that this kind of trespass
      must somehow be curtailed. Melissa nods and sobs.

Thirteen Ways of Looking at the Calendar

I. Oh, moon, as you pull the ocean,
    so you pull the tides of my body,

II. sometimes marshlands,
    squishy and fertile,
    sometimes running
    high with blood.

III. Back pain, belly pain—
     worth it when you
     deliver infant joy.

IV. Man and woman
    are one. Man and woman
    and baby are one.

V. But who tried to turn
    13 into 12?
    30 days hath September,
    et cetera. So much easier
    with 28. Example: If you get the
    Moderna vaccine on February 5
    in a non-leap year, you'll get the
    second one on March 5.

VI. Either approach, still winter
    chills the air. Summer still comes
    humming in.

VII. Oh, women of ancient China,
     you created a calendar
     honoring the silver of the moon
     and the red of your own blood.

VIII. And Gaelic tongues made
one word serve for two concepts:
"menstruation, *miosach*" and
"calendar, *miosachan*."

IX. The lunar calendar is consistent
each month but needs an extra
day each year to make the
solstices stick.

X. What other number inspires
such paranoia that it needs
a name? *Triskaidekaphobia*

XI. The flag of the United States has
13 stripes.

XII. The moon flips through her
phases. We all feel her.

XIII. Yin and yang search for balance.
Sunday and Monday can do the
same. *Mardi et Vendredi, aussi.*
Mars and Venus can, too.

II. Firebird on a Changing Globe

Oh, Gulf

*The Deepwater Horizon drilling rig exploded off the
Louisiana coast on April 20, 2010, killing 11 workers
and spilling about 210 million US gallons of oil.*

*Then as dawn brightened and the day broke
Grendel's powers of destruction were plain . . .*
—*Beowulf,* tr. Seamus Heaney

Oil painting   of turquoise dusk.
Sun setting   on salmon waves.

Scaly waters.   Scaffolding.
Giant, human-like form   floating
Balancing   a beacon.

At sea's floor   silica crust punctured.
Cement seal exploded,   spewing
underwater   tornados.

Sunset dot   a rouge of sun.
Rig figure   fire-masked.
Flame heads   flared.
Charcoal bones   collapsed, sank
wave-   wedded.
Real human   forms
plunge into   wet eternity.

Gaseous   gushing.
Then whole wards   of sheared fish.
Oiled pelicans turned   into earthworms.
Turtles,   my totems,
capsized,   dying in the slick.
Turtles, my link   to the Triassic.

What are   we? Cain's spawn
like Grendel?   ready to devour, befoul
all the rest   of creation?

Oh, gulf, forgive   our greasy stigmata
left on eons   of blue water.

Firebird Suite

1. Arts Program, 2003

> *We are here to show what people, even little children, can create.*
> *It's a shame our government is poised to destroy.*
> —Music Teacher, Oak Grove School

School arts assembly
on the eve of the Iraq war.
Music teacher speaks
to an audience of parents.
Children create rivers
with scarves and rhythms,
villages with song.

Later I scan
the broadcast,
x-ray of an invasion,
for tell-tale
silver streamers of
depleted uranium.

Nab the banned: sub: stance: deflect: defect:
of birth: of birds

2. Arts Program, 2011

School chooses *Firebird*
arts theme. Children
construct forests with xylophones,
turn their bodies into horses and birds.
Then Fukushima,
then memories of Chernobyl.
Fifth-grader Quinn writes,

A bird, all life on the tips of its wings.
If it flaps them, a giant earthquake
cracks the earth in two.

> *Who can: forget: the hearth heap: or: remember: the kin:*
> *ship of skin: and fin.*

Ukraine's Red Forest
begins to sing again,
sometimes through double
or crooked beaks.

Firebird, flitting,
racing, tracing
a way out, a way forward?
> *How to: reap reply.*

3. In Search of Story Serum

> *The Firebird in fairy tales is usually an object of a difficult quest, initiated by finding a lost tail feather, most often at the bidding of a father or king.*

Stories haven't saved us yet (except
Scheherazade, saving herself).
Still slip me a potion, sail me away
on a Kafka-craft, in search, in search.

> *It seems there is a tsar who can't abide
> the nightly loss of just one golden fruit
> from his royal grove. He sends his sons, one
> by one, at dusk to find the orchard thief.*

A library table as my craft,
a raft to ride me from the high seas
of my emotions. At least save me from
a melt-down thanks to the interruptions
of the couple at the desk nearby, loudly
(and badly) teaching and learning geometry.
Don't they know what's at stake?

> *Each son will say he kept his watch but sleeps
> then lies about it. Until Ivan, the youngest,
> anoints his eyes with dew, keeps vigil, observes
> a midnight sun appear, a flaming peacock
> which gobbles the radiant fruit.*

Ivan lunges and captures a single tail-feather torch.
And then the orchard thieving stops.
But the tsar burns for the rest of the bird.
He commands his sons, "Now, go bring me that feathered fire."

And I keep asking myself, "where is the map,
the blueprint, the key to the code?" It must be
here somewhere. Over that horizon. On that shelf.

Hard-hearted tsar: feathered fire: untethered fire: nuclear fire

4. At Sunset

> *The future can exist only when we understand the universe as composed of subjects to be communed with, not as objects to be exploited.*
> —Thomas Berry, *The Great Work*

I am trying to make the shape of
that cloud into a dragonfly
but, really, it doesn't look like one.
The only cloud that looks remotely
reptilian (I do think of dragons
as reptiles, even when they are insects)
is long and snake-like,
perhaps a feathered snake, which,
like all the clouds right now,
is the color of nectarines blended with cumulus.
I am trying to make the color of the sky
into the blue of the Virgin's mantle,
that shade of blue so precious,
made from ground-up Lapis lazuli,
or Egyptian blends of copper and sandstone.
But really, the sky is a much lighter
blue right now. It holds the deeper
blue in reserve, whistling Delft
for another twenty minutes or so.

But back to the non-dragonfly cloud.
It now looks more like a baby bird
fallen from its nest: unfledged, scrawny,
wings skeletal, a fire-bird chick
flattened against blue tile.

Tile fire blue

Fire Dragon

after the 2017 Sonoma County fires

I didn't see its fangs but
I smelled its breath.
I didn't feel its heat but
I saw its rufous belly, red wings,
the raven cloud of its thoughts.
Its claws ripped me but not
through my own flesh.
Rather through a mycelial network
in the interdependent root
system in this valley.
Through the spasm I feel when
another's tree house is yanked out.
How to deal with five thousand spasms?

The beast has folded its wings,
withdrawn its claws. Graven image,
black, red, voracious, do not leave me.
Stay singed in my mind.
I need to know you, know you
are ready to spring again.
Know safety as illusion.

Ravenous Water

after the Sonoma County floods, February 2019

Woman in her 60s
delivers papers.
Lonely, midnight work.
She thinks—"I need my check,
they need their news."
Even in flood.
3 a.m. she calls dispatch,
"My car is filling with water.
I'm on my roof." The line goes dead.

          On the dinghy,
          I had asked for a buddy,
          but signals got crossed.
          All meant to swim close
          and watch dolphins splash,
          arch their backs. Alone in the ocean,
          humans soon seemed as far
          as the iguana-riddled islands.
          Waves unruly. My life
          ring not secured.

          I still feel that fear
          of slipping under,
          thrashing farewell to breath,
          bloating and converting
          all that I am
          back into sea.

Swift water rescue team
follows digital breadcrumbs.
Firefighters wade, find
no one. Faint cry
near Riverfront Park.
Team swims 50 feet.
There she is, grasping a tree,
water at her throat.
One fighter hugs her wet and cold.
She lets go the dark embrace.

Monarchs

Gray sky enflames my daughter's red hair,
also, the red bottle brush. But the butterflies
have folded inward, their colorful sides
hidden. They look more like dead leaves:
well-camouflaged.

See that branch, no that one? See the stump?
The next tree back. Follow it halfway up.
No, more than halfway.
See a clump? That's them.

The caterpillars of this species are very
finicky eaters—they eat only milkweed. Of course,
young mammals have a strong preference for just milk.

The day before Halloween there are plenty
of princesses here at the park. In pink.
Dancing and laughing and looking through the spotting scope,
where one can see a few monarchs with their colors showing.

And then, by the side of the trail:
a brilliant orange insect,
with white spots, and black veins like stained glass,
lands on a feathery red bottle brush flower.
Together they make a blood-orange elixir.

Seeing the Light

in Panama

Blue morpho butterfly, what
can you teach me about metamorphosis?
I who long to let my hair flow down.
You who ornament the rainforest
with lapis. You who, wings-closed, appear
an intricate wood carving, but dull enough
to camouflage on a dead leaf.
You then open yourself up to pure cerulean
with black line edging as in stained glass.
Then you become an ultraviolet strobe light
flashing and wobbling through the trees.
You turn us into paparazzi scrambling for
a video to remember you by.
When we're in the truck, we keep
pace with you but this is just a tease
because now we're disarmed and bumping.
Morpho, my eyes well up with your colors.
Your wings, paper-thin,
are now tooled leather,
now a Sainte Chapelle blue,
mysteriously lit from within.

Wings

> ... It is the story of all life that is holy and good to tell and of us two-leggeds sharing in it with the four-leggeds and the wings of the air and all green things, for these are children of one mother and their father is one Spirit.
> —Black Elk, Oglala Sioux, "Black Elk Speaks"

Great horned owl is out after her bedtime
to socialize and take food from trusted trainers.
We are cordoned onto a path
playing our part as landscape, trying not to be more
rambunctious than the statuesque saguaro.
Owl flies over us from one trainer to another.
Owl settles on a branch,
wearing her well-groomed tweeds,
rotates her head, meets my eyes.
I see you, you see me.
I could be you, you could be me.
There is a watery contact
like a light hose or umbilicus.
I think I am more than saguaro to you now,
(nothing against saguaro.) But I am a being
with eyes. You and I are both beings with eyes.

>   They call it a "blind" so we can see but not be seen.
>   First the tractor comes, scattering a confetti of meat.
>   Then the red kites come like musical notes
>   dancing across the page of the sky.
>   Then they come close enough that one can see
>   the rust of their chests,
>   the stripes of their wings.
>   Big birds with a tin whistle of a cry.
>   The crows have learned their place—
>   to wait, while singing the bass notes.

What is my place?
Under a wooden awning,
witness to a spectacle, knowing
the history of an endangered bird.
Take me in your talons to where
I can see long views.
In the air—aaaah—
I see our small ball of blue, green yarn,
snarled in confusion. What will become
of it? In his tin whistle voice, he seems to say,
*My dinosaur ancestors fuel the hurricanes
and forest fires. Let the glowing lump of sun
and wind's wings guide you.*

In a Galaxy We Call Home

in Costa Rica

We arrive at a gleaming meadow,
sun and grasses interlaced,
edged with gumbo limbo trees
(aka tourist trees, pink and peeling, like me)
and a barbed wire fence.
We look up and see the sky weaving
the rags of rainclouds into its blue.
Then look in the trees! A troupe of squirrel monkeys
—small, with close-cropped red hair.
They charge gracefully along the wire,
their little hands and feet fitting perfectly between
the barbs, following hunger, following
family, following beauty, too?
Their faces, like mine, are a mask of surprise.
Their drive moves them along,
lickety-split, until they are, for me,
a memory.

Slothful

Sometimes I just want to be
a three-toed sloth, slow to
move, to digest, to think.
My hair steeped in
the close rainforest air,
would be thick and coarse.
I would lay my muppet head,
with its Lone Ranger eye mask,
on my soft bug-bitten arms and
let all the threats to our existence
and my way of life float on by. I'd take everything
slow, let the algae grow on my hair
to hide me among leaves. I'd eat salad all my days. I'd take
a nap right now and another and
another. I'd stop being so
nocturnal—I'd sleep all night
and half the day.
I might resemble a very round Buddha,
calm and present in the slow tick of moments.
Let humans come and be curious about me.
Let them point cameras at me,
hoping I will do something interesting.
Let me not worry about doing
anything interesting, just breathing
and being as much like a leaf as
possible. Maybe a cecropia leaf—
that 12-pointed star that shades
the forest and eventually drops to its
floor, shriveling to a parchment lace,
slowly mulching the soil again and again.

Between Hourglass and Sea

> *Hatchlings usually emerge from their nest at night or during a rainstorm when temperatures are cooler . . . The little turtles orient themselves to the brightest horizon, and then dash toward the sea . . . Lighting near the shore also can cause hatchlings to become disoriented and wander inland.*
> —Sea Turtle Conservancy

It is an hourglass,
this nest of sand
and more sand,
crowded with parchment shells
and my siblings.
Through bead-curtains,
Sun felt like a razor on new-hatched eyes.

But Moon! Split-sand-dollar-Moon
and luminaria Stars!
Those and surf cymbals coax me out,
carrying my own tarnished shell
onto Earth's crust,
pointing my head and stretching
the agéd folds of my young neck.

I twitch forward
past the nest of death,
with stamps of dogfoot
and self-seeking trails of ants,
past rapt coarse shrieks,
towards the drumroll of surf on Moon-sand.

I displace heaps of small crystals,
leaving my impression,
a zaggéd track toward
the shattering sound.

First slap of Saltwater
sets me back.
but mouths *ever* for me.
I track, track, then fall

homespun into salt-wet-shivers,
rapture-ravenous.
Air and Water are rattled into one;
my thistle heart darting like Stars.

Planet of the Apples

Thank goodness Eve broke the taboo about apples!
Or what would we in Sebastopol do in the summer?
Especially this year when we badly need
our apple a day in the time of the plague.
This tart and sweet fruit can capture our moods.

Planet Gravenstein may be Mars—or the moon.
Often striped like Jupiter, too,
lately with a very smoky atmosphere.

What better way to say, "I love you"
than with fruit resembling the heart?
Give it to the apple of your eye, or to a teacher.
Or you can perform open-heart surgery,
cut the *corazón* out of the apple, slice fruit into pie,
cook it into crisp or sauce and there you have it—
another open-hearted gift.

They say Johnny Appleseed was a friend
to the Natives and to animals.
That he shared stories, young trees
and cider even more than seeds.
That he spread the gospel of equality and animism.
That he looked out for all sentient beings, even insects.
That he was vegetarian and walked barefoot
from Pennsylvania to Indiana.

Let's spend less time in airplanes and cars.
Open up the apples of our hearts.
Revise the apple of our planet
to include fewer hurricanes and fires,
more trees, more fruit, more pies.

Madre de Dios River

On the tipping bus, on steep and ragged roads,
past stone walls and Dr. Seuss trees,
we approach the mountain pass
feathered over in mists.

Descending the other side, on foot, I find banquets of
        parrot-beak blossoms,
            clear-winged butterflies on orchid leaf landing pads,
            silver-backed tanager,
            golden-tailed oropendula with its hanging nest,
            paradise tanager, its aqua hedged with jade.

Sprouting curling ferns on my head like moss on the walking tree,
with its crutches of exposed roots, at last I find you, river.

In flat-bottomed canoes, across all your fifty meters' brown
    breadth,
skim me along on your breast, Mother of Infinity,
your banks brambled with Amazonian coral trees,
strangled with fig trees, bouncing with red   howler   monkeys.

On shoals, log-like black caimans.
White-necked herons   rosy spoonbills   strut and blink.

Hoatzin—throwbacks—(their chicks with clawed wings) are
    archaeopteryx.

Take me to that outpost, river,
with palm-thatched hut,
calamine beach.

To this rickety bench for river-watching.
Trees opposite watch back.

   A seed-eater sings
    the first few notes
     of Brahms's Lullaby.

Band of clouds purples
as night paddles in.

A lone bird
  with perfect tonguing
plays her pipes.

Earth Works

Galápagos

Lucky to visit a volcano, barely cooled into island,
At its base. a water cave, striped algae-green, amethyst-purple.

Frigate birds, red balloons at their throats,
evoke Groucho's brows with their wings.

Tan iguanas, jowls shaking with menacing grins, butt heads,
rub butts, wriggle the black cliffs into Greek vases.

Boobies who break-dance.
Pose in niches of virginal blue,
become arrows, diving for fishes.

There's a rocky outcrop with a standing census
of twenty penguins, in spite of warming waters,
primping plush feathers and down, white eyebrows.

That sea lion pup, typical toddler, ready to
take on the world, explores away from napping mom.
Calls down sun to sparkle off wet fur.

I get to snorkel in the greenish world
of the turtle, a traffic jam among waving fronds.
But steady flippers stroke with ease, poise, timing.

Meanwhile, some human Galapagueños,
whose erstwhile fishing livelihood is nixed,
for whom the tourist trade is bust not boom,
break into a study center full of timelines, maps,
carvings of local creatures—leave a tortoise
lynched and hanging from the rafters.
It could have lived a century more.

Don't be shocked. Our traffic jams, our traffic
in fossils, my jet fuel that brought me here
on this eco-adventure, imperil every bit of this.

A pod of dolphins is clad to match the blue-gray
waves. Plump as the dinghy I sit in, and
almost close enough to pet, they arch their spines
in aquabatic joy, surrounding me,
calling me, bounding.
How will I answer?

In Wilderness

a villanelle with lines from Handel's Messiah

Like sheep, we each turned to our own way,
deaf to each other and to animal kin, and
the voice that's crying in the wilderness.

I find myself in a blur of snow
bleakest blue along horizon's edge.
I've gone astray and turned to my own way.

And then a distant form, a shambling shape,
and sounds like moans and hollering,
a voice that's crying in the wilderness.

The bear is white and shuffles up to me.
She touches her nose to my nose, and kneels.
I wonder if she, too, has lost her way.

I climb her back, her bristles thick, well-greased.
Her back accepts me like a cub. I fit.
She lifts her voice again, and sings her woes.

Beneath her fur, I see her tough black skin.
Sure-footed with snowshoe paws, hairy toes,
she's suited to this place, is not astray.

We travel to the edge of crumbling ice where
four hundred miles to swim for food has made her lose
her cub. I hope I'm not too far astray.
This wilderness fills with cries. I must tell this tale.

Variations on a Theme of Green

O let them be left, wildness and wet.
   —Gerard Manley Hopkins, 1881

1. Grass, after years of drought, some days of rain and then sun
My eyes' first feast was green.
Perhaps this is the reason
that I can scarcely hold
the splendor of this herb,
this blaze of fire-green,
this sip of rain-fed grass.
But I will wear its dress,
and dance in its ballet,
aware this hue can't stay.

2. Spring Pastures
These fields of grass
please me to the point of pain
as if each leaf were a quill
injecting me with chlorophyll,
making me cry
green tears of joy.

3. Indeed, green is going, going, gone
Our planet's fever hasn't broken,
with few rains, while sun seems everlasting.
A chain of smiley sun-faces in the next forecast.
Grasses will turn prematurely tan and gray and,
come fall, fire dragons will rule the day.

4. Long may it reign
In the long-winded litany of family
appreciations, my little daughter said simply,
"I'm grateful for green."

III. Spirit of Justice

A New Quilt for Martin Luther King Jr.

James Earl Ray boasted, "I slew the dreamer."
Who was this man who killed my hero, MLK?
Ray stood in a tub in a flophouse and shot at the mountaintop,
that is, at the Lorraine Motel across the way.
All this happened in Tennessee, in Memphis town.
But Ray was Midwest Scotch/Irish/Welsh, a kind of quilt.

Makes me think of my grandma's background and her quilt
that still covers me when at night I turn into a dreamer.
It was pieced intricately in a small Illinois town
where my mother grew up. Things were not really ok,
and she told me, she couldn't wait to get away.
Of course, in Illinois there is nary a mountaintop.

King didn't mean that kind of mountaintop.
Nor did I mean a blanket when I first said quilt.
But it turns out that Ray was also from Illinois, by the way.
His many prison escapes and passports show he was a schemer.
My sister thinks our grandpa was a leader in the KKK,
and she's learned that Illiopolis was a "sundown town,"

meaning, "If you're black, by sundown you'd best be out of town."
See the kind of climbing some must do to get to their mountaintop?
You might have to prevail over depression as well as racism like
    MLK,
piece together income, self-respect, education like a quilt.
Or overcome nightmares, insomnia to become dreamers.
More and more our country seems to have lost its way.

If we let him, Martin will show us the loving, non-violent way.
Throughout this country, in every city, state, county and town
we have so many families and Dreamers
who crossed deserts, oceans, mountaintops,
to try to stitch together the pieces of a better quilt,
a safer life, while inheriting the potent legacy of MLK.

I once had a student who said, "He's my main squeeze, that MLK."
I struggle with my own history and weaknesses to find my way.
Can I love the pastel kaleidoscope and thrift of the quilt,
still absolve the guilt, make a difference in classroom and in town?
Maybe from there I'll find the path to my own mountaintop,
looking for the fresh, clean water that will help me grow dreamers.

The Story

after Joseph Zaccardi

The day's story the last day's story the story
of this country from the beginning a story
of pilgrims in May flowers seeking religious freedom
and coming to a new-to-them land and stealing
someone else's land and stories and proclaiming
this story as self-evident "all men are created equal"—
what could be clearer—and what's more
going to an old land and stealing bodies and
disappearing their stories families languages
bringing them to the new land where the supremacy
of Enlightenment ideals were tarnished by enwhiteenment and so
that day's story becomes the next day's story and on until today's
story of a Black man who wanted to touch the world
—known as a gentle giant school basketball football star stuck in a
   poor 'hood
with drugs until church-work took him to the twin cities
then maybe passing a counterfeit twenty for cigarettes
and being forced out of his car seated on the sidewalk
handcuffed with the help of three more police
laid out face against asphalt kneed in the neck until dead
the real counterfeit is the story that most in this country behave
as though "all men (read people for men) are created equal"
oft repeating "with liberty and justice for all" when
stolen peoples and peoples whose lands were stolen have a story
of having a neck too often mixed up with a knee a noose a hold or
   a foot.

Sanctuary

for the nine* who died at Emanuel African Methodist Episcopal Church in Charleston, South Carolina, some of whose relatives called for forgiveness for the murderer, who had posed as a worshipper but was a white supremacist there to kill.

All I have
    words
        names   of those lately in the light
    and the tonnage of my heart

    They were in a holy and said-to-be safe place
    their eyes until lately   wide,
    their thorn of struggle   acute or middling like most
    shells of their ears open

Seeing one's child or parent or spouse, sibling, friend
    black brown red pink maize
        crumpled to gray ash in minutes

All I would give
    to have us   never
        reenact   this
            again.

Hot morning, clouds fray in the blue,
flag dithers. A glistening crow ascends
    branch by branch on the pine
to the supposed-to-be   safe
        top of the tree.

After all that has happened
    keeps happening
        merciful folks can still call
clemency for the murderer.

But I call out to the rest of us
Do some   thing.   Whatever your   nonviolent   thing
do it   do it   for them
for others in the cross-hairs of this country's history.
Keep doing it.   Insist.
Insist on outcome.   On coming out   new.

* *Cynthia Hurd, Susie Jackson, Ethel Lance, De-Payne Middleton-Doctor, Clementa Pinckney, Tywanza Sanders, Daniel Simmons Sr., Sharonda Singleton, Myra Thompson*

Scattered

Very clearly, violence is a huge driver of why these kids and other Central Americans are coming . . .
—Lisa Frydman, of Kids in Need of Defense

They are unquiet angels of this age.
Groomed with wind thorns,
their baby talc is desert dust.
Some ride their nightmares
on train roofs like river rafts.

Some drag a garbage bag
with change of clothes.
Most are soda bottle-fed,
those bottles refilled with
whatever fluids: sewage,
diesel-laced water.

They come accompanied or alone.
On these shores, rude stores of manna,
cages for the refugee.

Scatter the letters,
but will they speak truth.
Shatter the sun-
glasses of the masters of force
—can't they see at least darkly
what is plain—
the human vessel,
containing pain.

Like José, sobbing over
the stick figure "foto" of his family,
his mustachioed papá
forcibly split from him at the border,
before he was flown to a Minnesota "home."

Like Andres, always training one eye
on the person in charge,
the other looking for
his now-vanished mother,
his brother with bullet holes,
his sister's ghost.

Asylum is no longer asylum but abuse
—domestic, gang, political—is still abuse
Unquiet angels of this age.

Un Niño Que Ha Llorado

Día de los Muertos, 2018, the year when thousands of immigrant children were separated from their families at the border. 2018, año en que a miles de niños inmigrantes los separaron de sus familias en la frontera.

At the time of year of the dying sun,
when the time of day was night,
in a year when many families were un-membered,
we met for the Day of the Dead.

Día era noche and
I stood with my student before the crowd
*en la fiesta del Día de los Muertos, rodeados
de papel picado azul y rosado,* beloved faces in frames, sugar
    skulls.

Con mi alumno, ante la multitud,
I read of my own mentor who gave up her ghost in May.
Surrounded by paper lace, framed faces, *calaveras de azúcar,*
my boy, reading homage to his grandma, cried, could not go on.

Hablé de mi mentora, que siento que aún me sigue.
Reading of his *abuela*'s empty bed,
el niño se atragantó, no pudo continuar.
I read the end—about the fire of his grief.

La cama de su abuela ahora vacía,
his aunt materialized beside him, held him.
El fuego de su dolor aún lo consumía.
but we all began to dance, to conjure:

nuestros seres queridos se materializaron a nuestros lados
as we ate bread of the dead, drank *horchata* like mother's milk.
*Evocamos amigos, padres, mentores para que bailaran con
   nosotros otra vez*
Later, many told me the boy's tears had crystalized their loss.

*Comimos pan de muertos, bebimos horchata como leche materna,
en la época del año del sol moribundo.*
Para muchos, las lágrimas del niño hicieron cristalizar su pérdida
in a year when families more than ever needed re-membering.

Asylum Seekers

for the African refugees

Like so many shadows, they streamed aboard.

One degree　　more　　of sunshine
and all impulses
of strength and energy would wither
under　a sinister　　splendor of sky.

With a hiss, and a white ribbon of foam,
pilgrims　　　　progress
across　　a blaze of ocean
shed　　upon the earth.

Days disappear over a bridge
bounded by prone bodies, prayer
carpets, deck chairs, tin coffee pots

into an abyss.

The sea a perfect level, perfect circle—
　　　black speck of ship everlastingly? at its center.

Eyes did not see the shadow of the coming event.
Black fingers letting go
a twist of the body
in the white streak of the wake.

Deportation 1 (out of 975 so far)

Since the coronavirus broke out, the Trump administration has deported hundreds of migrant children alone—in some cases without notifying their families.
   —Caitlin Dickerson, NYT 5/20/20 (an erasure poem, with two letters added)

son   Gerson
        Be good   behave
Border Patrol other side of   river
      uncle in Houston
10-year-old   squinty smile   tears caught in dimples

raft   across Rio Grande

Expected: Gerson would be held Border Patrol few days
    then transferred   shelter for migrant children
    brother in Houston   would claim him

    Gerson   disappeared
six frantic days   nothing

    Finally   panicked phone call
    cousin in Honduras
      Gerson with her

little boy crying   disoriented   confused
    ended up back in   dangerous place

uncle   shocked: Gerson sent back alone
    worried about safety partner had beaten boy and
  mother, withheld food
      put a child on a plane?   without
notifying family?
      home   welcome   he deserved

Among Many Days of the Dead

*June 12, 2016, when a gunman shot and killed 49 individuals at Pulse,
a gay and Latinx night club, in Orlando, Florida*

Two slender men—
with tan bodies,
tank tops, tattoos—
console, embrace
like trees entwined.
These two telegraphed
the story on national news
and endure
in the grove of my mind
above a scattershot of the fallen.

Can I speak the names behind the names?
      Angel, Beloved, Bread-and-Water, Carrier,
      Daughter, Defender, DJ, Earth Worker, Farm.

Angel wings shielded mourners from protesters
(protesting LGBTQ existence)
as they made their way to funerals.
Many opened veins and gave
until banks overspilled.
Rainbow flags flowered.
Matches scratched and leapt
into flame, into candle.

      Flaming Sword, Fortress, Guard, Holder, Healer,
      King, Listener, New House, Painter, Ruler, Young Mother.

Thinking of my children, my students, and the forty-nine,
I have made pilgrimage to an ocean full of blue and salt.

    Of course there were at least two Frank Ones, two Humble
        Ones,
    Warriors one, two, three and four,
    the Gracious, Generous, Gracious, Generous ones,
    the Strong, Blessed, Just, Kind, God-like ones,
    Priceless, Priceless.

What have I done with these Gifts of God?
        Forest, Wolf, Bear, River, Forest, Wolf, Bear, River,
        Deer, Snow, Deer, Snow, dear Sea-and-Sun,
        dear Sea-and-Sun, dear Clearing, Rock, Rock, Rock—
on this Rock I will build
        more *Muertos* altars. These still overflow.

Lumps

for George Floyd

I never knew the man.
But his face is painted brightly on my psyche
as it is on so many murals around the world
—in Minnesota, Kenya, Berlin, Houston.
He looked like he already had a lump
in his throat, one of kindness, compassion,
before his throat was fatally knelt on by
someone who didn't.

I imagine a lump in my breast,
like the one my mother had, dread diagnosis.
Definitely, a lump in my heart, not smooth,
but a jagged, heavy rock.
A lump in my breath that falters on his behalf.
A lump in my rest that I can't climb over
and get past, night after night—
makes me want to escape to sleep right now.

But still I see his face.
I wish it could be a mirror for his daughter
so they could look into each other's eyes,
or on a teddy bear she could play with,
or on a shield that would protect her—
in short, the father that she will
grow up without.
I still see his face.

Dear Editor

for Christine Blasey Ford

There's my grandma waving from the train window,
Smart, probing. What was a girl like that,
born in the 1880s, to do? Write letters,
some to newspapers, teach
Sunday School. When she died,
I hid a few letters in the attic of her house
so something of her would remain.
She speeds past.

There's me at 24 in therapy.
The couch flashes past like a train car.
The girl is bright, insecure, not pretty.
The therapist is her father's age,
promises sexual liberation, freedom from
self-doubts. Says he knows what she wants,
what she's wanted for a long time. She thinks,
I do? I have? The train speeds along,
driven by a patriarchal God.

I see a train car paneled like the Senate hearing room,
and Dr. Blasey Ford raising her hand,
swearing her truth, shy but certain
in the chambers of power, like
Susanna of the book of Daniel.

There's Susanna covering herself with her shawl
while the lecherous elders leer, plot to extort favors.

There are Rebecca Nurse and Martha Corey of Salem,
shaking their heads, loosened by the noose.

Anita Hill presses her face to the glass
to see if anything in the landscape has changed.

I see myself in the window of my laptop,
typing, typing. Writing letter after letter.
One for grandma, another for mom,
one for auntie, one for each daughter,
sister, girlfriend.

All the letters are for the women on this train,
or anyone carrying these scars.

Like a speeding train, I aim letters to papers
across the country, trying to ghost write a reckoning.

Christine (Blasey Ford)

I tried to put Truth in a cage!
—William Carlos Williams, "The Fool's Song"

You preferred a quiet nest,
a continent away from corridors of power,
but the fate of justice
was at stake, and you sang out.
The world and I now know your secret.

You were direct as a sunbeam
in those paneled Senate chambers,
while the accused zigged
and zagged, bullied and blustered.

He now is robed and elevated.
Robes hide a lot of sins
but some are turning to cellophane now.

    (My secret shows up on an x-ray of my past that you enabled.)

Remember:
big lies are loud, but
the bird of truth
often breaks its cage.

Congressional Pirates?

An interview with Filibuster about the elusiveness of gun reform

Phyllie: What is your history, Filibuster?
Filibuster: *Who, me? Who wants to know?*
P: Me. I'm Phyllie, buster.
F: *You mean my name then?*
P: Well, let's start there.
F: *It seems to have come from Dutch, "vribuyter,"*
meaning free booty or loot. It made its way through French,
(filibustier) to Spanish (filibustero) whence it came to the Americas,
 but likely all of this was based on English's freebooter or
  fleebooter.
If you'd said my name back in the early 1850s you would have been
referring to an irregular military adventurer, or a pirate,
often responsible for stoking insurrections.
P: Interesting. How 'bout in politics in the U.S.?
F: *Though he used a different name for me, Aaron Burr advised that*
I become part of the rules as of 1806 but I was never used for thirty years.
P: Aaron Burr, he's the one who killed Alexander Hamilton, right? (Now there's bipartisanship!) So, the founders didn't include you in the Constitution?
F: *I'm not in there at all. I was just used*
a handful of times in the first one hundred years.
P: When did you become such a big shot, and I mean in particular in defeating gun reforms?
F: *Well, that's complicated. In the 1970s, rules changed allowing the Senate to consider more than one subject at a time. Senators can toggle among topics.*

There's no need for cloture—or voting to cut off debate. Sometimes you can't even <u>start</u> debate!
P: Well, that's a nice goal for the "world's most deliberative body!"
F: *So, after Sandy Hook, there was a bipartisan majority for universal background checks. But it wasn't a big enough majority to satisfy me. It was only 55 to 45 and nobody had to debate or even say a word. It was just quietly defeated by a minority representing only 38% of the American people.*
P: Wow! Doesn't sound like democracy to me.
F: *One of my proudest exploits . . .*
P: Enough said.
F: *Oh, yeah? Back in the day—or even now, if I wanted to—I could read through state laws, recite old speeches, share my favorite recipes, talk about my favorite movies . . .*
P: Speaking of movies, I see that nowadays you're nothing like Mr. Smith in *Mr. Smith Goes to Washington.*
F: *Yes, that's true. Silence can be golden.*
P: I hear there's talk of reforming you back to more the way you used to be—having to talk. What do you think?
F: *I don't know . . . I'm not as glamorous now, but way more effective!*
P: Kids in their classrooms are being blown to bits by weapons meant for the battlefield. Don't you think the federal government has a duty to intervene?
F: (Filibuster gets up and heads for the door.)
P: Wait. You didn't answer my question.
F: (Speaking over his shoulder as he leaves the room.) *I don't have to. I'm Filibuster!*

End of interview.

A Book of Ruths

My mother's name was Ruth—
Ruthie at affectionate moments
from Dad. *Ooie,* originally
from the neighbor baby who
couldn't yet say her *R*s,
then for years used in a playful way.

Less than 30 years after women
had gained the right to vote,
Mom lay in a hospital bed in Illinois,
when the fall leaves were glowing bright,
having just given birth to me.
She had to beg to get a ballot—absentee.
If those Republican doctors had known
how I was going to vote,
they never would have agreed,
she once mused. It was a close
enough election that *The Tribune* got
the headline wrong the next day.
But, in truth, her candidate had prevailed.

Mom died a couple years after RBG
was seated on the Supreme Court.
I know she must have felt relief
at someone in power who knew feet
were on the necks of women. Justice
Ruthie was about the same height
as my mom, a little thinner,
born a couple decades later,
but she, too, knew how women had been
undermined and misused for millennia.

RBG was asked what the right number
of women on the Supreme Court would be
and she answered—I thought I heard *none*
at first, but it was definitely *nine*. Spunk.

Mom had sweetness and some spunk.
RBG had both in spades. Spunk in defense
of equal rights under the law. *Ut sit.* May it be so.

Jokes

Did I tell you my father was a highly respected professor?
That he was a professor of English literature at an esteemed
   university?
Did I tell you he held wit-jousting matches with his colleagues at
   the U?
That at home he would paraphrase Samuel Johnson, saying
  "a woman preaching is like a dog dancing—the noteworthy thing
  is not whether it's done well but that it is done at all"?
Did I tell you that he would quote his father's "wisdom?"—
  "Why give women the vote?
  They'll just vote the way their husbands tell them to."
That he said these things at home in front of my mother, chief cook
   and bottle washer,
  designer of the dining room, and the gourmet meals and parties
  that brought his career to fruition?
Did I tell you that his idea of a joke was, when a guest
   complimented
  my mom on her cooking, to say, "Thank you" with a flourish?
  Prompting queries about whether he was really the chef
  to which he replied, "Well, we twain ARE one flesh!"

I Promise

for the students at Jhilod School, Jhilod, Gujarat, India

I promise I will remember you,
children seated in the school courtyard.
One girl, quick in her stillness, eyes now penetrate from pictures.
Three girls from third standard, eyes tight,
fingers ringed in *O* mudra,
mouths making *O* for *Om*.
Five boys talking drum
seated at our visiting feet.
Six girls dancing
to the thump and tinkling of drums,
their saris dyed by dusk and papaya,
desert sky and neem leaf.
Six girls, bringing us floral tributes,
touch our feet, request a blessing
from our hands to their heads.

Eighty children seated on flagstones
singing up at us in Gujarati, singing into English,
god's love is wonderful, it is over all and under all.
Eighty children quietly accept the candies
we lean down to present,
returning any that fall, guiding
us to visit their schoolmates all.

I promise I will remember
your schoolroom, its blackboard
drywall crawling with chalk cuneiform
I cannot read. Thirty children
sit cross-legged on tile floors, listening
to their barefoot teacher.

I promise. I have given you my word
in the language of group photos and hugs.

Mouse of Enlightenment

Who knew?
You who use up batteries much faster than I'd like,
who are probably the reason for my shoulder's ache.
But, yes, you nose around into subjects of great import.
"Who was that unarmed Black man recently killed by police?"
Click. Then I know a number of their names: George Floyd,
Kajieme Powell, Philandro Castile, Rumain Brisbon,
Michael Brown, Iberia Parrish, Laquan McDonald,
Chavis Carter, Eric Garner, Kenneth Chamberlain,
Kendrec McDade, Rekia Boyd, Orlando Barlow,
Daunte Wright, Tyre Nichols, Ronell Foster . . .

Mouse, what do you do at night when computer is asleep?
Do you really stay on your tiny mouse pad?
Are you in solitary confinement?
What if those Black men had not been killed
but instead locked up? I guess
that mind-damaging arrangement would be
slightly better because where there's life,
there's some hope, but still . . .

Oh, mouse, please help us.
You know what? Let's look up John Lewis,
that share-croppers' son who met hate with love,
who turned a broken skull into a nest for problem-solving,
34-year veteran of the House, the "Conscience of the Congress."
Let's see if he can give us an idea of what to do
that will take our country someplace new, more just.

Notes on the Poems

Page 27, "Morning, Galápagos Islands:" German physician Friedrich Ritter and his mistress Dore Strauch immigrated to Floreana Island in the Galápagos Archipelago in 1929, and Heinz and Margaret Wittmer did so in 1932. Books like *The Galapagos Affair* have explored the suspicious deaths and disappearances of Ritter and other Floreana inhabitants.

Page 34, "Erysikthon:" In Theoi Greek Mythology, a Thessalian king who chopped down the sacred grove of the goddess Ceres and her nymph in order to build himself a feast-hall.

Page 36, "Mothers, Daughters, Sisters:" Epigraph spoken by Apollo in defense of Orestes, who was accused of killing his mother.

Page 84, "Asylum Seekers:" Based on passages of Joseph Conrad's "Lord Jim" chapters 2 and 3.

About the Author

Phyllis Meshulam is Poet Laureate Emerita for Sonoma County, California, a county with a population comparable in size to that of Wyoming.

During her 2020–2022 tenure, she conceived of and coedited *The Freedom of New Beginnings,* an anthology of poems from across the county and beyond on issues of justice and sustainability.

She is author of *Land of My Father's War,* winner of an Artists Embassy International Prize, 2019, published by Cherry Grove Collections. Joy Harjo, US Poet Laureate, said of Meshulam's book, an "urgency of spirit has emerged eloquently here in these poems of perception and even prophecy. . . ." Meshulam has authored four other titles, and she taught for California Poets in the Schools for 21 years. She also edited CalPoets' *Poetry Crossing,* which *Poetry Flash* called "a joyful collection of lessons and poems."

She has an MFA from Vermont College of Fine Arts and a BA from Pomona College.

Made in the USA
Columbia, SC
22 February 2025